GROUNDCOVER
SERIES

Text research: Richard Ashby

Acknowledgements

Liverpudlians are famed for their friendliness and I have been almost
overwhelmed by the help and hospitality offered whilst working on this book.
Total strangers have plied me with countless cups of coffee, suggested sites
I should visit, moved cars and even helped collect offending litter. I thank you all.

My appreciation extends to John Ashby, Les Birchall, The Crown, Angela Dixon,
Liverpool Central Library, Local Studies and Archives, Mayfield Estate
Management, Simon Paine, Bernadette Potts, Robert Reddaway,
Six Continents Retail Ltd. (Philharmonic Hotel), The Vines,
Father Stephen Webb and Peter Wilson.

Special thanks go to Richard Ashby for his special commitment to this project,
Caroline Jarrold, Malcolm Crampton for suggesting the title, Sarah Letts,
Sonya Calton, Kaarin Wall and all at Jarrold Publishing.

John Curtis

Front cover picture: Ferry on the River Mersey
Back cover picture: St George's Square

Designed and produced by
Jarrold Publishing,
Whitefriars, Norwich NR3 1TR

All photographs
© John Curtis

© Jarrold Publishing 2002

ISBN 0-7117-2078-9

Printed in Belgium.

1/02

PUBLISHER'S NOTE
Variant and archaic spellings have
been retained in quoted material,
while the modern spellings of
place-names have been used in
headings.
  The inclusion of a photograph
in this book does not necessarily
imply public access to the building
illustrated.

Liverpool

JOHN CURTIS

LIVERPOOL

GROUNDCOVER
SERIES

Liver Bird

Contents

PIER HEAD

Most lunch hours I walk down to the Pier Head to see the ships, the Mersey and the sea. The air there is always fresh, sometimes a little too fresh for me, but it brings a smell of the sea which is one reason why I like Liverpool.

GEORGE CHANDLER *Why I Love Liverpool* 1960

Introduction

Liverpool is best approached 'across the water', preferably on the world famous ferry. The city stretches beckoning along the east bank of the grey, swirling waters of the River Mersey, the trio of Pier Head buildings, with the monumental Royal Liver Building, comfortably familiar even to those visiting for the first time, taking centre stage. The centre of the city climbs almost imperceptibly in a series of plateaux behind, while rising over all are the contrasting towers of the two great cathedrals. Here, without question, is one of the world's great cities.

Liverpool was England's second port, boasting trading links with North America, the West Indies, Europe, Africa, China and India. It was here in 1840 that Samuel Cunard established the first shipping line carrying passengers to North America.

Trading connections brought an eclectic mixture of races and traditions from the four corners of the world, each contributing to Liverpool's rich and unique culture – the city has the oldest established Chinese community in Europe.

The meteoric rise of Liverpool's status and wealth in the eighteenth and nineteenth centuries has also left an enviable architectural heritage. There are more listed buildings here than in any other English city. Many buildings, most notably warehouses and dock buildings on the river front which until recently lay abandoned and facing demolition, have been transformed into shops, offices, museums, cafés, bars and even television studios. Liverpool is also probably the most verdant of our major cities with over 2,600 acres of public parks. Prince's Park, the first independent commission of Joseph Paxton, the architect of the Crystal Palace, in 1842 was the earliest, while Birkenhead Park, on the other side of the Mersey, was the first municipally funded park in the world. Also designed by Paxton, it influenced Frederick Olmsted's designs for Central Park in New York.

The world's attention was again focused on Liverpool in the early 1960s when the 'Mersey sound' hit the airwaves. Suddenly there was a 'British Invasion' of America, led, of course, by The Beatles. It seemed that fame was assured for anyone who could strum a guitar, play the drums and/or sing, but more importantly, had a broad 'Scouse' accent. The Beatles, Billy J. Kramer and the Dakotas, The Searchers and Cilla Black are all names indelibly forged into the annals of popular music history. Fans from all around the globe still make pilgrimages to Liverpool to visit the Cavern Club in Mathew Street, forever identified as the home of Mersey Beat.

While the shelter in the middle of the roundabout in Penny Lane is reputed to be the most photographed structure in Liverpool, this multi-faceted city offers infinite possibilities for the photographer, the artist and the writer. This book takes us on a photographic and literary tour, leading us first around the city centre, then around the equally interesting outlying areas, finishing with a brief excursion across the Mersey to Birkenhead and lovely Port Sunlight. I hope these images manage to capture just some of the many aspects of this remarkable city.

JOHN CURTIS

ST GEORGE'S HALL

The many fine buildings of modern Liverpool are perhaps seen to better advantage than those of any other place in the county, the middle or business part of the city being laid out with fine streets and culminating in a 'stately piazza, with its spread of statues and temples and other solemn Athenian things in the St George's Hall plateau'.

F. H. CHEETHAM
Lancashire (Little Guides)
1920

STATUE OF DISRAELI
ST GEORGE'S PLATEAU

Upon the steps Disraeli stands,
That idol of the Primrose Bands,
Where every true Disraeli-ite
Performs his primrose-laying rite.

MAUD BUDDEN
From 'St George's Hall: An Instructive
Rhyme for The Youth of Liverpool'
1932

STATUES OF QUEEN VICTORIA AND PRINCE ALBERT
St George's Plateau

Two equestrian statues of bronze representing the late Prince Consort and Her Majesty the Queen, stand in front of St George's Hall, each on a granite pedestal. The first, which is that of his Royal Highness, sitting in an easy attitude, hat in hand, perhaps receiving an address, or listening to the cheers of a loyal assemblage, bears, on one side of the pedestal, an inscription, 'Albert, Prince Consort; born 1819, died 1861'; on the other side, 'This statue of a wise and good Prince was erected by the Corporation of Liverpool, October 1866.'…The companion statue of Her Majesty…was unveiled in November, 1870. It presents the Queen on horseback, as she used to appear occasionally reviewing some of her troops.

Illustrated London News
15 May 1886

CENOTAPH
St George's Plateau

An old woman I saw at the
Liverpool cenotaph carrying
poppies and wearing the medals
her son had won on the fields of
Flanders, told me that she had
lived for this day, when Liverpool
would remember her son. 'Jack
will sleep more peacefully in his
grave in France now' she said,
'and I shall have somewhere to
bring him flowers.'

She didn't weep as she spoke
these words; she just seemed
satisfied that her boy had come
into his own in his native city.

Liverpool Echo
11 November 1930

Reported on the unveiling of the
Cenotaph, St George's Plateau.

WELLINGTON MONUMENT
William Brown Street

…upon a column 118 feet high, is
a statue of the Duke of
Wellington, art from cannon
captured at Waterloo, a material
poetically meet for the
perpetuation of the outward
form of such a man…

Harper's New Monthly Magazine
January 1879

FORMER **NORTH WESTERN HOTEL**
LIME STREET

Mr Badger, manager of the London and North Western Hotel, has found the American and Canadian passenger traffic to Paris and London much heavier this year than it has been before. Upwards of four hundred travellers can be accommodated at the North Western Hotel at a push but…scores of people have had to be refused accommodation at present…

The Liverpool Review of Politics, Society, Literature, and Art 1889

LIME STREET STATION

[Lime Street station had the first]railway-station roof to be constructed as a single span…The single span and absence of columns permitted certain changes to the layout of platforms and tracks to be made much more easily (and more flexibly), removed awkward obstructions in the platforms, and reduced the unlikely but dreadful possibility of a rogue engine careering into a column and bringing the whole structure down on the station.

JAMES STEVENS CURL
Victorian Architecture
1990

CROWN HOTEL
LIME STREET

One of Liverpool's most decorative pubs…Exceedingly heavily decorated, almost theatrical, Victorian interior, mostly in wonderfully vulgar maroon and gilt. The ceiling is also worth a glance as you slide under the table and the whole place looks more like a theatre than a pub.

The Liverpool Book
1989

ST JOHN'S
GARDENS

At one time the site of St John's Church, demolished in 1898, was favoured for the proposed new Anglican Cathedral, but the proximity of St George's Hall and the importance of retaining this city centre open space met with serious objections, and gardens for rest and refreshment were created instead.

PICTON LIBRARY
WILLIAM BROWN STREET

You can't make a noise in the Picton,
They won't stand a clatter or brawl.
You must ask for your books
With intelligent *looks*
Or you won't get a volume at all.

You can sing in the City Museum,
You can prattle away to the seal,
You can welcome the sight
Of each mummified fright
With a perfectly natural squeal…

But you can't make a noise in
    the *Picton*,
You can't even splutter or choke.
If you ventured a cough
It might blow the dome off
And that would be more than a joke.

MAUD BUDDEN
From 'The Picton: A Cautionary Rhyme'
1932

LIVERPOOL MUSEUM William Brown Street

…the cluster of fine public buildings surprised them very much indeed and one of the visitors remarked that she had seen nothing superior since she left Athens.

Two Foreign Ladies give their opinion of Liverpool 1890

WALKER ART GALLERY
William Brown Street

The Walker Art Gallery contains some wonderful old pictures, as well as many fine works of modern artists. It…should be visited by all who are fond of beautiful things, or care to learn the lesson they can teach. Some of these old pictures were painted between four and five hundred years ago, in Italy, the land which has given the world its best paintings. They may appear strange and unlifelike, until we have learned to understand something of their meaning. Then we shall feel that to possess them is a privilege of which any city may be proud.

EDWARD ARNOLD
The Story of Lancashire
1896

WHITECHAPEL

The commercial buildings
erected of late years have much
of a palatial character, and are
certainly not below those of
Genoa, Turin, or Venice…

J. A. PICTON
Memorials of Liverpool
1875

STATUES OF KING GEORGE V AND QUEEN MARY
MERSEY TUNNEL ENTRANCE (QUEENSWAY)

My wife and I are very glad to be
able to come here to-day to
unveil the statues of my father
and mother, whose names will
always be associated with the
Mersey Tunnel…I know what an
impression the great engineering
work made on my father, and
how pleased he was to perform
the opening ceremony.

THE DUKE OF KENT
On the unveiling of the statues of King
George V and Queen Mary at the entrance
to the Mersey Tunnel
1939

…although the enormous prosperity of Liverpool may be stigmatised by some as a plant of very recent growth, we cannot forget that the town has a history of singular interest, is at the present moment the largest, wealthiest, and most prosperous in England next to London, and has before it a future which promises to be equally grand with its past.

The Graphic
5 May 1877

RIGBY'S
DALE STREET

It was a peculiar feature in all the houses owned by Mr Rigby that barmen were employed in preference to barmaids, and strict rules were laid down for their guidance in conducting the business.

CHARLES MILLWARD *Old Liverpool Snuggeries* 1889

QUEEN AVENUE

…Liverpool, in spite of herself, and quite unconsciously, is a place of exceeding beauty. Out of that hard turmoil of tangible interests and endeavours a very splendid and reassuring happening has sprung. In honest and shrewd response to instant necessities, the city has been carved and kneaded into the lean lines of practical effectiveness; and those lines have joined wonderfully together to make any number of unpremeditated glories. Loveliness has descended unawares.

DIXON SCOTT
Liverpool
1907

VICTORIA MONUMENT
DERBY SQUARE

One meets it almost full blast; not quite, however, for strangely enough it is not quite central…It looks as if it had been gently pushed aside to make way for the tramcars. The dome, half on and half off its columns, adds to the illusion, as does Sir Oliver Lodge struggling with his young men to keep his precarious seat.

C. H. REILLY
Some Liverpool Streets and Buildings in 1921
1921

CASTLE STREET

If Bold Street is our pleasantest street, Castle Street is certainly our noblest. It is of a fine width, with good broad pavements on either side, and its length is not too great. It is a great disadvantage, as one notices in America, for streets to go on endlessly. Castle Street is definitely closed and presided over at one end by the Town Hall and its dome.

C. H. REILLY
Some Liverpool Streets and Buildings in 1921
1921

TOWN HALL

The dinner was at the Town Hall, and the rooms and the whole affair were all in the most splendid style. Nothing struck me more than the footmen in the city livery. They really looked more magnificent in their gold-lace and breeches and white silk stockings than any officers of state. The rooms were beautiful; gorgeously painted and gilded, gorgeously lighted, gorgeously hung with paintings, – the plate was gorgeous, and the dinner gorgeous in the English fashion.

NATHANIEL HAWTHORNE
English Notebooks
August 1853

EXCHANGE FLAGS

…for long a pedestrian concourse and in past centuries a centre of commercial trading. It has been said that slaves were regularly sold here but there appears to be little truth in the story which may have had its origin in chained figures, a striking feature of the monument to Nelson that adorns the Flags.

HOWARD CHANNON
Portrait of Liverpool
1972

NELSON MEMORIAL
EXCHANGE FLAGS

THIS monument did Liverpool erect
The mem'ry to eternize and protect
Of far-famed NELSON, England's naval
　　pride
Who in the midst of glorious victory died.
And see, where figured forth by artist's
　　hands,
The image of the noble warrior stands;
Whilst awful emblems compass him around,
By DEATH arrested – and by VICTORY
　　crown'd!

BEHOLD! the HERO calmly yields his
　　breath,
And smiles on VICTORY, tho' he's seized by
　　DEATH!
While VICTORY crowns his sword – but
　　could not save
The illustrious HERO from the lowly grave.

ELLEN ROBINSON
From 'Poem on seeing the Monument Erected
at Liverpool to the Honour of LORD NELSON.'
1823

INDIA BUILDING
WATER STREET

…she stands to-day second to none as a municipality, a shopping centre without equal outside the Metropolis, and famous for her broad streets and noble buildings.

The Story of Liverpool: The Second City of the Empire
1925

The India Building, an enormous office block constructed in 1923, contains this impressive arcade in which the little shops retain their original fronts and discrete signs.

ORIEL CHAMBERS
WATER STREET

It is a sort of honeycomb of numberless plate-glass oriel windows held together by a stonework skeleton frame designed to look like cast-iron…Its humour as a cellular habitation for the human insect is a distinct asset to its town.

C. H. REILLY
Some Liverpool Streets and Buildings in 1921
1921

CHURCH OF OUR LADY AND ST NICHOLAS
CHAPEL STREET

St Nicholas is the Patron Saint of sailors and the Parish Church of Liverpool is known as the Sailors' Church. It has witnessed many events in its long history, none more tragic that the death of 23 charity school girls, killed by the collapse of its tower in 1810 when the bells were being rung.

MERSEY FERRY

Fare you well the Prince's
    landing stage,
River Mersey fare you well
I'm off to California
A place I know right well.

So fare you well my own
    true love
When I return united we
    shall be.
It's not the leaving of
    Liverpool that grieves
    me. But my darling
    when I think of you.

From 'The Leaving of Liverpool':
Nineteenth-century sea shanty

ROYAL LIVER BUILDING AND CUNARD BUILDING
PIER HEAD

Feeling the pulse of this city
that moves and shapes itself
in the contours of the future,
solidly rooted in the present –
a dreamed-up city of fantasy
shining with the works
of its people, their strength
their humour and endurance.

W. A. MARSHALL
From 'Envoi'
1985

ROYAL LIVER BUILDING
PIER HEAD

Respecting the etymology of its
name, various opinions have
arisen; but although the subject
still remains a matter of doubt, it
is generally believed to be derived
from a fabulous bird called the
Liver; and this accordingly figures
in the arms of the town.

*Liverpool as it is: or a Guide for the Stranger
and Resident…*
1854

MERSEY DOCKS AND HARBOUR BOARD BUILDING
PIER HEAD

Wherever men of the sea gather, from Singapore to San Francisco, the name of the port that smacks most of their trade is Liverpool on the muddy banks of the Mersey.

> Blow him away to
>   Liverpool town,
> Oh, give me some time to
>   blow the man down.

Liverpool! Irresistibly romantic name.

WALTER GREENWOOD
Lancashire: County Books
1951

RIVER MERSEY

This mighty city, ocean-kissed and free, stands like a beacon in the golden west, And welcomes to its bosom from afar, The sons of commerce riding o'er the sea.

Thy sons and daughters hail thee from afar, And send thee greetings from across the main, wishing thee increased trade, good luck, and wealth, With happier days to all who 'cross Mersey's bar!'

HENRY SMITH
Liverpool

ST GEORGE'S DOCK VENTILATION AND CENTRAL STATION OF THE MERSEY ROAD TUNNEL

Each of the (ventilating) buildings has achieved a monumental character of a new type, and they are indeed symbols of the philosophy of an architect [H J Rowse] who is open to new ideas, but has the will and ability to adapt them to the needs of the particular problem in hand.

Building
May 1934

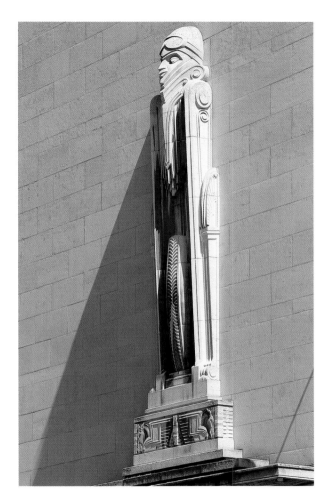

ST GEORGE'S DOCK VENTILATION AND CENTRAL STATION OF THE MERSEY ROAD TUNNEL

Carved in high relief, the figure represents speed…it is an extremely stylized, tall, streamlined figure, wearing a motor racing helmet with raised goggles. Apart from the head, all human characteristics are eliminated from the slender block to emphasize the long, vertical lines which are intended to convey motorized speed. On the central axis of the figure, up to waist height, is a wheel, represented edge on – as if a motor bike is racing over the viewer's head.

TERRY CAVANAGH
Public Sculpture in Liverpool
1997

ALBERT DOCK

…we were shown the enormous building going on at the new dock (Prince Albert's dock) which is to be surrounded with splendid warehouses. A million pound sterling has been set aside for the building of this dock. The basin is almost finished, and a number of warehouses completed…That the corporation of the town, which is building all these works entirely at its own expense, should show them with considerable pride may well be imagined, but I found their pride fully justified.

Dr C. G. CARUS
The King of Saxony's Journey through England in 1844
1846

SALTHOUSE DOCK

On the sides of the docks are warehouses of uncommon size and strength, to the different floors of which goods are craned up with great facility; whilst the space around the docks is sufficient to give room for the loading and unloading of the ships, which lie with their broadsides to the quay, and for the different occupations of sailors, and the crowds of passengers, without confusion or interruption.

The Stranger in Liverpool or an Historical and Descriptive View of the Town of Liverpool and its Environs 1823

RIVERSIDE WALK

Warehouses! that to
    commerce vowed
Still know the grace of sun
    and cloud,
Through pearly mist and
    slender rain
I read strange beauty in
    your plain
Void walls, a grey serenity
That's earnest of the quiet
    sea…

RACHAEL BATES
From 'Sea Change'
1923

TATE GALLERY
ALBERT DOCK

What is to be done with large areas of warehouses and docks, made redundant by the changing needs of modern commerce? Liverpool was one of the earliest places to recognise the potential for the new use of old buildings. The result has been a most successful transformation from dereliction to new life with television studios, museums, offices, shops, housing, restaurants and the superb collection of modern art in the Tate Gallery.

ENTRANCE TO CANNING HALF TIDE DOCK

The town now has an opulent, flourishing and increasing trade, not rivalling Bristol, in the trade to Virginia, and the English island colonies in America only, but is in a fair way to exceed and eclipse it, by increasing every way in wealth and shipping. They trade round the whole island, send ships to Norway, to Hamburgh, and to the Baltick, as also to Holland and Flanders; so that, in a word, they are almost become like the Londoners, universal merchants.

DANIEL DEFOE
A Tour Through the Whole Island of Great Britain
1724–6

ALBERT DOCK

Their cargoes unnumbered, both
    common and rare,
Their bales and their gunny sacks,
    tea chests and cases,
From all kinds of countries and
    all sorts of places,
Their copra and teakwood, their
    rum and their bacca,
Their rice and their spice from
    Rangoon and Malacca,
Their sugar and sago from far
    Singapore,
And lumber and logwood and
    manganese ore.

Cox's Merseyside Annual: The Authoritative Year Book of Industrial Merseyside
1930

CHURCH HOUSE
HANOVER STREET

…as one of the world's great
ocean terminals, Liverpool
serves as a home at sometime
or other for many of the great
cargo ships that roam the
seven seas, and the sailors, be
they from Callao or Calcutta
are as much part of the local
scene as they are on their
native waterfronts.

JOHN COWLEY
Liverpool as I see It
1965

Church House was formerly
the Central Institute of the
Mersey Missions to Seamen.

ALBION HOUSE
JAMES STREET

'A slice of New Scotland Yard' is the common criticism on the White Star offices…

It is difficult to over estimate the good such a building as this must do in a town. That it is not universally admired is a tribute to its boldness and originality, and a proof that it is a real work of architecture.

Architectural Review 1900

The Who
Paul
The Beatles
John
The Rolling Stones
Pickett
Gerry & The Pacemakers
Ringo
George
The Big Three
Nazareth
Stu
Pete
Queen
Tubby Hayes
Clyde Valley Stompers
Wishbone Ash
Billy May
Budgie
Shane Fenton & The Fentones
Alan Price Set
Undertakers
Chuck Berry
The Kinks
Fourmost
Status Quo
Suzi Quatro
Freddie Starr & The Midnighters
Alexis Korner Blues Inc.
The Shadows
John Mayalls Blues Breakers
Georgie Fame & The Blue Flames
Gene Vincent
Spencer Davis Group
Little Eva
Rod Stewart
Oasis
Judas
Rory Storm & The Hurricanes
Sony Webb & The Cascades
The Merseybeats
The Moody Blues
Elton John

MATHEW STREET

The people remain confident, amusing and resourceful; the football teams beat everybody and the music is as fresh, interesting and influential as ever. It's the music that grabbed me and made me stay!

CON McCONVILLE
From the introduction to *The Scouse Phenomenon: The Scrapbook of the New Liverpool Rock Scene*
1987

CAVERN CLUB
MATHEW STREET

Because Liverpool has never been a particularly fashionable place to be from, no one ever really cared about the manner in which the Scouses talked until two years ago when four local lads climbed out of a onetime warehouse called the Cavern Club and spread the sound around the world. Then something wonderful happened to Liverpool.

Newsweek
14 December 1964

ST JOHN'S BEACON

The landmark is as much a part of Liverpool skyline as the Liver Birds and as well known in the city as Pier Head or St George's Hall. Impossible now to imagine, to remember, Liverpool without that slim shape…

Liverpool Daily Post
9 April 1970

PLAYHOUSE THEATRE
WILLIAMSON SQUARE

With justification it has been stated that the Liverpool Playhouse has enriched the stage to quite an extraordinary extent, and that probably more of our best actors and actresses have learned their art in Williamson Square than in any other part of the country, many of them never looking back after departing to other locations.

HAROLD ACKROYD
The Liverpool Stage
1996

FORMER BLUECOAT SCHOOL
SCHOOL LANE

Little Bobby Barton, with his little
    white cravat,
And his long-tailed coat, and his flat
    blue hat,
Has started on the path to
    knowledge.
  He is walking down the Lane
  With his little sister Jane,
For they've just joined the Blue
    Coat College.
  She wears a big poke bonnet
  With a broad blue ribbon on it,
And a neat white tucker on her long
    blue gown.
    And they're trying to be cheerful,
    But they're really rather tearful,
For they can't help feeling lonely in
    Liverpool town.

EVELINE SAXTON
From 'School Lane'
1948

CLAYTON SQUARE
SHOPPING CENTRE

This stylish shopping centre is reminiscent of the iron and glass arcades popular in Victorian England.

LYCEUM
BOLD STREET

The Lyceum is a handsome structure…
It was erected by public subscription,
at an expense of upwards of £11,000.
The proprietors are 800 in number,
whose annual subscription is one
guinea each. The news-room…is well
furnished with London, provincial,
and foreign newspapers, and with a
variety of magazines, reviews, maps,
&c. The library…contains upwards of
21,000 volumes.

The Imperial Magazine
March 1821

THE VINES
('BIG HOUSE')
LIME STREET

The other day a friend said to me
'You ought to be proud to be a
citizen of Liverpool, for Liverpool
will one day be the Florence of
the North.'

CHARLES CARTER
The Florence of Tomorrow
1934

THE VINES
('BIG HOUSE')
LIME STREET

…no bibliophile should leave
Liverpool before quenching
his thirst in either the Vines
in Lime Street, or the
Philharmonic in Hope Street.
The Vines is a gin palace of the
most splendidly ornate
Edwardian baroque at its
finest with a sumptuous
interior of mahogany,
mirrors, and cut glass.

J. E. VAUGHAN
A Brief View of Liverpool
1966

ADELPHI HOTEL
LIME STREET

Dear Mr Forster,

I wrote you last night, but by mistake the letter has gone on Heaven knows where in my portmanteau. I have only time to say, go straight to Liverpool by the first Birmingham train on *Monday Morning* and at the Adelphi Hotel in that town you will find us.

I trust to you to see my dear Kate, and bring the latest intelligence of her & the darlings. My best love to them.

In the utmost haste
Always your faithful friend
CHARLES DICKENS

The Letters of Charles Dickens,
vol. 1, 1820-1839
2 November 1838

'LIVERPOOL RESURGENT' JOHN LEWIS DEPARTMENT STORE
RANELAGH PLACE

The statue is the thing. It symbolises Liverpool's future, this unmistakably male nude, Liverpool Resurgent, nay Tumescent. It stands for our virility. It is larger than life, I'll say, by Epstein…

It caused a sensation when it was unveiled. It is said Lewis's shop-girls threatened to walk out – they weren't going to work under a … like that! … A councillor friend said to me: 'Why cudden they put it in the Art Gallery whur nobody would see ut?'

FRANK SHAW
My Liverpool
1971

ABERCROMBY SQUARE

…the remains of Abercromby Square remind us of the old aristocratic Liverpool of stately Georgian houses.

From 'England's Gateway to the Western World, The Wonderful Second Port of Empire'
1931

SEYMOUR STREET

All the new parts of Liverpool are regularly laid out with straight and wide streets, some of them truly handsome. The material is for the most part brick.

J. AIKIN
A Description of the Country from Thirty to Forty Miles round Manchester
1795

METROPOLITAN CATHEDRAL OF CHRIST THE KING

As you enter the cathedral you must ask yourself if the architect has understood the function of a Catholic cathedral. The glorious light coming from the mighty tower may be the first striking feature but the light itself is focused and poured down upon the altar itself.

FREDERICK GIBBERD
Metropolitan Cathedral of Christ the King
1968

Liverpool's Roman Catholic cathedral was designed by Frederick Gibberd in 1960 and was consecrated in 1967.

METROPOLITAN CATHEDRAL OF CHRIST THE KING

The fact that it has become the subject of innumerable jokes suggests that it has been amiably accepted by the people of Liverpool who already look upon it with affection. Its giant wig-wam is splendidly photogenic and the building is undoubtedly the major modern architectural attraction of the city.

QUENTIN HUGHES *Liverpool: City of Architecture* 1999

VICTORIA UNIVERSITY BUILDING
BROWNLOW HILL

University College, designed by Alfred Waterhouse, was built in the middle of the nineteenth-century Gothic revival and is a queer mixture of elements. But it is also solid and not without dignity.

From 'England's Gateway to the Western World, The Wonderful Second Port of Empire'
1931

VICTORIA UNIVERSITY BUILDING
BROWNLOW HILL

The man who lives in a large town has always at command a source of instruction and entertainment, of counsel and of warning. If he have no books let him sally forth into the streets, and he will find the whole town a large volume, richly stored with information, and open day and night for his perusal.

HUGH STOWELL BROWN
Twelve Lectures to the Men of Liverpool
1858

RODNEY STREET

The famous victory of Lord
Rodney over the Comte de
Grasse on June 2nd 1780,
is still commemorated in the
signboards of many a country
town, and has given the name
of our gallant sailor to many
a street and alley.

JAMES PICTON
Memorials of Liverpool
1875

RODNEY STREET

Mr Gladstone was born in
Rodney Street, and the present
occupant of the house says that,
being desirous of placing the
matter beyond doubt, and for
the satisfaction of future
generations, Mr Gladstone was
asked by him if this were indeed
where he was born, and replied
– characteristically on a post
card – that it was.

ROBERT MACHRAY
Liverpool Illustrated
1896

William Ewart Gladstone was
British Prime Minister four
times in the reign of Queen
Victoria.

CHURCH OF ST LUKE
ST LUKE'S PLACE

St Luke's Church at once arrests the eye of admiration by the boldness of its design and beauty of its execution. Its architect, John Foster, Esq. has been certainly most successful, and has reared a pile highly creditable to his talents. Viewed from the side it exhibits a harmony of purpose that cannot be too much praised.

Gore's Liverpool Directory and Views of Liverpool and its Environs
1832

RODNEY STREET

Our Squares are no longer fashionable. Like Rodney Street, their interest lies mostly in their memories; yet good evening parties may still be enjoyed there…

B. GUINESS ORCHARD
Liverpool's Legion of Honour
1893

DEAN WALTERS BUILDING
JOHN MOORES UNIVERSITY, CATHEDRAL GATE

On a sensitive site at the approach to the Anglican Cathedral, the new building for the John Moores University successfully links elegant Georgian with heavy Gothic.

CHINATOWN

I love Liverpool like other people love Paris, New York, or sweet and sour pork.

PRISCILLA HODGSON
From 'My Liverpool'
1964

FORMER ST JAMES'S CEMETERY

It is a dell, which was formerly a quarry, and it is one of the most beautiful and suitable places that could well have been found for the solemn purpose to which it is set apart…In the area of the cemetery there are numerous elegant monuments, some of which bear impressive inscriptions, all of them affectionate ones, and beautiful flower beds planted over graves give pleasing testimony to the sorrow of grieving relatives and friends.

Whitty's Guide to Liverpool
1871

ANGLICAN CATHEDRAL CHURCH OF CHRIST

The visitor who takes his stand at the corner where Hope Street joins Upper Duke Street, will gain some idea of the commanding situation and splendid possibilities of the site, which in many respects recalls the beauties of Durham and Lincoln. St James's Cemetery lies at its foot, and the wooded hillside, some 50 feet in height, leading up to the summit of the Mount, will add beauty as well as dignity to the noble building which is to crown the eminence.

CHARLES HARRIS
The Building of the new Liverpool Cathedral: its History and Progress
1911

ANGLICAN CATHEDRAL CHURCH OF CHRIST

…I am convinced that the Cathedral, whose foundation-stone it is my great pleasure to lay today, will minister to the spiritual needs of this great community, and will form a noble addition to the architectural adornments of your city.

KING EDWARD VII
On the occasion of the laying of the foundation stone
19 July 1904

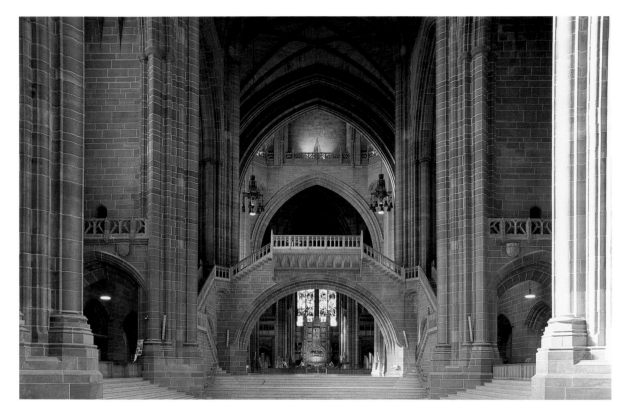

GAMBIER TERRACE

There are great differences of level in the various parts of the town, so that many of the streets climb steeply from one to another. Owing to this variety of elevation many of the principal buildings are seen to great advantage.

PETER FLEETWOOD-HESKETH
*Murray's Lancashire:
Architectural Guide*
1955

ANGLICAN CATHEDRAL CHURCH OF CHRIST

Liverpool Cathedral is the largest Anglican cathedral in the world – St Paul's, in London, is only half the size. It has the highest arches, the largest organ and the heaviest bells.

Former LIVERPOOL INSTITUTE SCHOOL
Mount Street

Both Paul McCartney and George Harrison were pupils at the school. The building, with its modern extension, is now the Liverpool Institute for the Performing Arts, and Sir Paul McCartney attended the official opening in 1996 and has lectured here.

BLACKBURNE HOUSE
Blackburne Place

Here, a hundred years ago, the comfortable Liverpool merchants lived, going in and out of these charming doorways and beneath these fine old fanlights, thinking about their cargoes of cotton and tobacco from New Orleans and of rum and sugar from Jamaica.

J. B. PRIESTLEY
English Journey
1934

PHILHARMONIC HALL
Hope Street

The Philharmonic Hall, Hope Street…was erected in 1849 for providing a building where the finest music might be presented by the best *artistes* before audiences which were growing year by year more wealthy, numerous, and luxurious, but until then possessed no really suitable building acoustically perfect, with retiring rooms, appropriate auditorium, and freedom from vulgar interference.

B. GUINNESS ORCHARD
Liverpool's Legion of Honour
1893

HOPE STREET

…The streets are faire and long, its London in miniature as much as ever I saw any thing.

CELIA FIENNES
The Journeys of Celia Fiennes
1698

PHILHARMONIC
HOTEL
HOPE STREET

A large and very impressive
Edwardian Gin Palace…Interior
fitted out by ships carpenters laid
off from building liners, so that
now you have the excuse for going to the pub to do research into early twentieth-century naval architecture. It is the only place that I
know of that has stained glass windows all over it (including one of Baden Powell) and marvellous Carrara marble urinals in the gents…

The Liverpool Book 1989

CANNING STREET

In a word there is no town in England, … that can equal Liverpool for the fineness of the streets and the beauty of the buildings. Many of the houses are built of freestone, and completely finished; all the rest (of the new part) of brick, as handsomely built as London itself.

C. CRUTTWELL
Tours through the Whole Island of Great Britain
1801

PERCY STREET

Miss G – observed in our way 'that Liverpool was a place, which would suit a person who chose a residence of less bustle than London, and more tumult than Bristol…'

A Sentimental Journey by a Lady is in The Lady's Magazine
1775

GREEK ORTHODOX CHURCH OF ST NIKOLAOS
PRINCES ROAD

A surprising find in the city, Byzantine architecture is a rarity and here it contrasts strongly with its more mundane surroundings.

LITTLEWOODS' BUILDING
EDGE LANE, WAVERTREE

From small beginnings in 1924, when John Moores started his football pools, Littlewoods grew rapidly, with both mail order and a chain of high street stores, to become the largest employer on Merseyside.

EDGE HILL STATION
TUNNEL ROAD

The buildings, which are here placed on each side of the line, are of uniform elevation, and consist of two engine-houses for the fixed engines…a dwelling, which is occupied by W. Ralph, who attends the engines; a booking-office and waiting-room in one; a lamp-shop, and also porter's lodge and dwelling.

FRANCIS WHISHAW
The Railways of Great Britain and Ireland,
Practically Described and Illustrated
1842

CROXTETH HALL
CROXTETH COUNTRY PARK

This magnificent mansion, with its majestic Queen Anne west wing, is the centre of the 500-acre Croxteth Country Park, now in the care of Liverpool City Council.

AINTREE RACECOURSE

The Steeple Chase on Wednesday formed what many considered ' a fair excuse' for leaving the town and business for a few hours, in order that they might breathe the clear air 'with freshness spring laden' and 'crush the sod' upon the meadows at Aintree…It need never be supposed that half of the multitude assembled at the course last Wednesday, went simply from the interest that they felt in the horse-racing or steeple-chasing. Many scarcely saw the horses; and others who did see them did not know anything about them…They came out for fresh air, and the excitement which a crowded course always creates helped to give a fillip to it.

The Porcupine 15 March 1862

WOOLTON

…the village of *Woolton*, pronounced *Wooton*; where is a pleasant villa at the farther end, with a fine prospect. A comfortable dinner, &c. may be had at *Mrs Denton's*; where from the bowling-green, the prospect may be advantageously enjoyed.

W. MOSS
The Liverpool Guide including a Sketch of the Environs, with a Map of the Town and Directions for Sea Bathing
1799

THE BLACK BULL
GATEACRE

As Liverpool expanded it absorbed a number of villages nearby. Although often surrounded by nineteenth- and twentieth-century housing and other developments, some, like Gateacre, retain their character and their charm.

FORMER SPEKE AIRPORT TERMINAL BUILDING

Since the recent inauguration of the city's airport at Speke, this new arm of service has developed with unexpected rapidity, and regular daily air services are now operating...More than half a dozen services now use the aerodrome every day.

Extensive new buildings and accelerated transport from the aerodrome to the city are among the immediate improvements at Speke, which the City Council has resolved shall be abreast of the best aerodromes in Europe.

Where to Go, What to See and Where to Stay in Liverpool
1934

The Speke Airport Terminal building is now a hotel.

SPEKE HALL

The old building has happily since Jacobean times been left almost unaltered, and is one of the finest and richest specimens in the district of the 'black and white' or half timbered method of construction.

HENRY TAYLOR *Old Halls in Lancashire and Cheshire including notes on the Ancient Domestic Architecture of the Counties Palatine* 1884

CHURCH OF
ST AGNES
ULLET ROAD

A baby Truro Cathedral but
without the central tower
and spire…But it is certainly
not small in scale…It is 19th-
century architecture in 13th-
century dress, but still
unmistakably Victorian.
One of the most impressive
churches in the city…

QUENTIN HUGHES
Liverpool: City of Architecture
1999

CALDERSTONES
PARK

…like a fleck of pure foam far
cast by the muddy wave of
the town, lie the lawns and
gardens of Calderstone, the
latest of Liverpool's parks.

DIXON SCOTT
Liverpool
1907

STRAWBERRY FIELD
BEACONSFIELD ROAD, WOOLTON

The inspiration behind the song 'Strawberry Fields' has long been a popular place for Beatles fans across the world. Many visit the legendary gates, behind which is the garden where John Lennon once played as a child.

251 MENLOVE AVENUE
WOOLTON

Mary Elizabeth Smith and her husband George, who owned a local dairy, would become as close to a real mother and father as John [Lennon] would ever know. They lived in a small, spotlessly clean, semi-detached house at 251 Menlove Avenue.

PETE BROWN and STEVEN GAINES *The Love You Make: an Insider's Story of The Beatles* 1983

20 FORTHLIN ROAD
ALLERTON

…the two of them [Paul McCartney and John Lennon] spent long afternoons together at Paul's house in Forthlin Road, practising songs, teaching each other chords, and raiding the pantry for jam butties. Sometimes they'd play standing in the tub in the tiled bathroom to get a better echo.

PETE BROWN and STEVEN GAINES
The Love You Make: an Insider's Story of The Beatles
1983

SMITHDOWN
PLACE
'PENNY LANE'

This corner of suburban Liverpool has become world famous through The Beatles song. There is still a barber and a bank, but the bus shelter is now a restaurant.

SEFTON PARK

…a most surprising place to find in the heart of a noisy seaboard town. It has ponds and groves, a Peter Pan garden and secret winding ways. In the heart of the park is a dainty palm house, with great banks of tropical colour and gleaming statuary and delightful figures outside…

From 'England's Gateway to the Western World, The Wonderful Second Port of Empire' 1931

CHURCH OF ST MICHAEL IN THE HAMLET

St Michael's Church was built in 1815…Mr. Cragg of the old 'Mersey' Ironfoundry, Tithebarn Street, was concerned in its construction…Much of the detail of this beautiful building is of iron cast at Mr. Cragg's foundry. The ornamental work of the steeple, the numerous pinnacles, the various mouldings on the exterior and the dado round the outside, are of cast iron; this has earned for this edifice the synonym of The Cast Iron Church.

R. GRIFFITHS
The History of the Royal and Ancient Park of Toxteth, Liverpool
1907

PRINCE'S PARK

All honour to the man whose benevolence devised and whose perseverance carried out the scheme. His memory deserves to be held in grateful remembrance…Altogether the Prince's Park forms a very agreeable suburb. Houses of a high class nestle among the plantations. Bright green undulating lawns sparkle in the sun, and within the same distance from a crowded town it would be difficult to find a pleasanter locality.

J. A. PICTON
Memorials of Liverpool
1903

BIRKENHEAD PARK

Laid out in 1843-7 by Sir Joseph Paxton, The Duke of Devonshire's gardener at Chatsworth who became famous as the designer of the Crystal Palace, Birkenhead Park was the first park to have been provided at public expense for the enjoyment of the people. As the first of its kind, its design was very influential in the development of other public parks, including Central Park in New York.

HAMILTON SQUARE
BIRKENHEAD

…Hamilton Square is rated as one of the finest provincial squares in Europe.

PETER HOWELL WILLIAMS
Liverpolitana: a Miscellany of People and Places
1971

PORT SUNLIGHT

[William Lever, later Lord Leverhulme] had observed the effects of people living in overcrowded conditions, seeing little in the way of daylight, with little or no space to call their own. He now conceived the idea of a 'garden village' for the workers – 'cottages' pleasing to look at, and comfortable to live in, set in wide, curving roads planted with lawns, trees and shrubs. This indeed would be a Port Sunlight in every sense of the words.

KENNETH J. BURNLEY
The Illustrated Portrait of Wirral
1987

LADY LEVER ART GALLERY
PORT SUNLIGHT

Port Sunlight has done all things well. We walk about it and see beauty everywhere. Yet it has one crowning gem, its beautiful two-domed Art Gallery, build by Lord Leverhulme in memory of the woman whose help never failed him in all those years of building up. We wonder if there is anywhere a more attractive place of its size that the Lady Lever Art Gallery.

ARTHUR MEE
The King's England: Cheshire
1968

We also present and finde that there is in Toxteth Parke a certaine chappell, called Toxteth Chappell, and that Mr Huggon is minister there, and is an approved minister, and hath for his salarye or maintenance the proffits of the tythes of the said towne or hamlett, which we conceive to be worth cleerly ffortye-five pounds pr annum…and that the said chappell of Toxteth Parke is farr distant from an other church or chappell, and therefore wee think it very fitt to be made a parish…

From a report by Parliamentary Sequestrators 1650

Acknowledgements

Every effort has been made to secure permissions from copyright owners to use the extracts of text featured in this book.

Any subsequent correspondence should be sent to Jarrold Publishing at the following address: Jarrold Publishing, Whitefriars, Norwich NR3 1TR.

17 (left) From the *Liverpool Echo*. Reproduced by kind permission of the Liverpool Daily Post and Echo.

18 (right) From *Victorian Architecture* by James Stevens Curl. David and Charles, 1990. Reproduced by kind permission of the author, Professor Stevens Curl.

20 (left) From *The Liverpool Book*. Woodrust Ltd, 1989.

27 (right) From a speech given by the The Duke of Kent, reported in *Liverpool Daily Post*, 1939. Reproduced by kind permission of Liverpool Daily Post and Echo and St James's Palace.

37 (left) From *Portrait of Liverpool* (2nd edition) by Howard Channon. Robert Hale Ltd, 1972. Reproduced by kind permission of the publisher.

42 (left) From 'Envoi' by W. A. Marshall in *Liverpool Medley: Poems of Location*, 1985.

44 From *Lancashire County Books* by Walter Greenwood. Robert Hale Ltd, 1951. Reproduced by kind permission of the publisher.

49 (left) From *Building*, May 1934.

49 (right) From *Public Sculpture in Liverpool* by Terry Cavanagh. Liverpool University Press, 1997. Reproduced by kind permission of Liverpool University Press and Public Monuments and Sculpture Association (PMSA).

53 (left) From 'Sea Change' by Rachael Bates in *Poets of Merseyside: an Anthology of Present-Day Liverpool Poetry*, selected and arranged by S. Fowler Wright. The Merton Press, [1923]. Reproduced by kind permission of the Senate of Liverpool University.

59 (top) From the introduction, by Con McConville, to *The Scouse Phenomenon: The Scrapbook of the New Liverpool Rock Scene* by Klaus Schwartze. Drucker und Verlag Bitsch GmbH., 1987.

59 (bottom) From *Newsweek*, vol. 64, No. 24, 14 December 1964.

60 (left) From report in *Liverpool Daily Post*, 9 April 1970. Reproduced by kind permission of the Liverpool Daily Post and Echo.

60 (right) From *The Liverpool Stage* by Harold Ackroyd. 1996.

63 From 'School Lane' by Eveline Saxton in *Rhymes of Old Liverpool*. Liverpool Daily Post, 1948. Reproduced by kind permission of the Liverpool Daily Post and Echo.

66 (right) From *A Brief View of Liverpool* by J. E. Vaughan. Reproduced by kind permission of the author.

68 (right) From *My Liverpool* by Frank Shaw. Wolfe Publishing, 1971.

73 (left) From *Metropolitan Cathedral of Christ the King* by Frank Gibberd. Architectural Press, 1968.

73 (right) From *Liverpool: City of Architecture* (second edition) by Quentin Hughes. The Bluecoat Press, 1999. Reproduced by kind permission of Professor Quentin Hughes.

81 (right) From 'My Liverpool' by Priscilla Hodgson in *Liverpool Daily Post*, April 23, 1964 . Reproduced by kind permission of the Liverpool Daily Post and Echo.

85 (right) From a speech given by King Edward VII. Reproduced by kind permission of Chief Correspondence Officer, Buckingham Palace.

86 (right) From *Murray's Lancashire: Architectural Guide* by Peter Fleetwood-Hesketh. John Murray, 1955. Reproduced by kind permission of John Murray (Publishers) Ltd.

89 (bottom) Reproduced from *English Journey* by J. B. Priestley (Copyright (c) J. B. Priestley 1934) by permission of PFD on behalf of the Estate of J. B. Priestley.

93 As 20 (left).

106 (left)) As 73 (right).

109 (right) From *The Love You Make: an Insider's Story of The Beatles* by Pete Brown and Steven Gaines. Macmillan, 1983.

110 As 109 (right)

117 (bottom) From *Liverpolitana: a Miscellany of People and Places* by Peter Howell Williams. Published by Merseyside Civic Society, 1971. Reproduced by kind permission of Dr Williams.

118 (left) From *The Illustrated Portrait of Wirral* by Kenneth J. Burnley. Robert Hale, 1987. Reproduced by kind permission of the publisher.

118 (right) From *The King's England: Cheshire* by Arthur Mee. © The Estate of Arthur Mee and the King's England Press.

Bibliography

Ackroyd, Harold: *The Liverpool Stage.* Printed by Amber Valley Print Centre, 1996.

Aikin, J: *A Description of the Country from Thirty to Forty Miles round Manchester.* John Stockdale, 1795.

Architectural Review. Vol. 8, 1900.

Brown, Pete and Gaines, Steven: *The Love You Make: an Insider's Story of the Beatles.* Macmillan, 1983.

Bates, Rachael: *Sea Change* is in *Poets of Merseyside: an Anthology of Present-Day Liverpool Poetry,* selected and arranged by S. Fowler Wright. The Merton Press, 1923.

Brown, Hugh Stowell: *Twelve Lectures to the Men of Liverpool.* Gabriel Thomson, 1858.

Budden, Maud: *St George's Hall: An Instructive Rhyme for The Youth of Liverpool* is in The Liverpolitan: a Monthly Review of Merseyside Affairs, July, 1932.

Budden, Maud: *The Picton: A Cautionary Rhyme* is in The Liverpolitan: a Monthly Review of Merseyside Affairs, October, 1932.

Building. May, 1934.

Burnley, Kenneth J: *The Illustrated Portrait of Wirral.* New Edition, Robert Hale, 1987.

Carter, Charles: *The Florence of Tomorrow* is in the Liverpool Evening Express, May 15, 1934.

Carus, Dr. C. G: *The King of Saxony's Journey through England in 1844.* Chapman and Hall, 1846.

Cavanagh, Terry: *Public Sculpture in Liverpool.* Liverpool University Press, 1997.

Chandler, George: *Why I Love Liverpool.* 1960. Typescript in Liverpool Record Office and Local Studies Library.

Channon, Howard: *Portrait of Liverpool* (2nd edition). Robert Hale, 1972.

Cheetham, F. H: *Lancashire (Little Guides).* Methuen & Co Ltd., 1920.

Cowley, John: *Liverpool as I see It* is in Illustrated Liverpool News, Vol. 9, No. 69, December, 1965.

Cox's Merseyside Annual: The Authoritative Year Book of Industrial Merseyside. John Furness & Co. Ltd., 1930.

Cruttwell, C: *Tours through the Whole Island of Great Britain.* C. and J. Robinson, 1801.

Curl, James Stevens: *Victorian Architecture.* Newton Abbot, David & Charles, 1990.

Defoe, Daniel: *A Tour Through the Whole Island of Great Britain 1724-6.* Abridged and edited with an introduction and notes by Pat Rogers. Penguin Books, 1971.

Dickens, Charles: *The letters of Charles Dickens, Vol. 1, 1820 – 1839.* Edited by Madeline House & Graham Horey. Clarendon Press, 1965.

Edward VII, King. The speech on the laying of the foundation stone of Liverpool Anglican Cathedral is in Charles Harris: *The Building of the New Liverpool Cathedral: its History and Progress.* Published by the Cathedral Committee at the Church House, 1911.

England's Gateway to the Western World, The Wonderful Second Port of Empire is in My Magazine, November, 1931.

Fiennes, Celia: *The Illustrated Journeys of Celia Fiennes, c. 1682-1712.* Edited by Christopher Morris. Macdonald, 1982.

Fleetwood-Hesketh, Peter: *Murray's Lancashire: Architectural Guide.* John Murray, 1955.

Gibberd, Frederick: *Metropolitan Cathedral of Christ the King.* Architectural Press. 1968.

Gore's Liverpool Directory and Views of Liverpool and its Environs. J. Gore and Son, 1832.

The Graphic. 5 May, 1877.

Greenwood, Walter: *Lancashire: County Books.* Robert Hale, 1951.

Griffiths, R: *The History of the Royal and Ancient Park of Toxteth, Liverpool.* [No publisher], 1907.

Harper's New Monthly Magazine. Vol. lviii, no. cccxliv. January, 1879.

Harris, Charles: *The Building of the new Liverpool Cathedral: its History and Progress.* Published by the Cathedral Committee at the Church House, 1911.

Hawthorne, Nathaniel: *Our Old Home and English Notebooks.* Kegan Paul, Trench and Company, 1883.

Hodgson, Priscilla: 'My Liverpool' is in *Liverpool Daily Post*, April 23, 1964.

Hughes, Quentin: *Liverpool: City of Architecture* (2nd edition). The Bluecoat Press, 1999.

Illustrated London News. Vol. lxxviii, No 2456. 15 May, 1886.

The Imperial Magazine, or *Compendium of Religion, Moral, & Philosophical Knowledge.* March, 1821.

'Liver Bird', St George's Dock Ventilation and Central Station of the Mersey Road Tunnel

Kent, Duke of: The speech on the unveiling of the statues of King George V and Queen Mary at the entrance to the Mersey Tunnel, July 7 1939, is reported in the *Liverpool Daily Post*, July 8 1939.

The Leaving of Liverpool: Nineteenth Century Sea Shanty was found at http://wwwfeniks.com/skb/music/lull11.html

*Liverpool as it is: or a Guide for the Stranger and Resident…*9th edition. Edward Howard, 1854.

The Liverpool Book. Woodrust Ltd., 1989.

Liverpool Daily Post 9 April 1970 (supplement).

*Liverpool Echo.*11 November 1930.

The Liverpool Review of Politics, Society, Literature, and Art. Vol. xx. No. 1082. August 31, 1889.

McConville, Con. From the introduction to Klaus Schwartze: *The Scouse Phenomenon: The Scrapbook of the New Liverpool Rock Scene.* 1987.

Machray, Robert: *Liverpool Illustrated, Gates and Pillars of the Empire, No 1. Liverpool Illustrated,* in Pearson's Magazine, April 1896.

Marshall, W. A: 'Envoi' is in *Liverpool Medley: Poems of Location.* Pip Instant Printers, 1985.

Mee, Arthur: *The King's England: Cheshire.* First published 1938, fully revised and edited by E. T. Long. Hodder and Stoughton, 1968.

Birkenhead Priory

Millward, Charles: *Old Liverpool Snuggeries.* Liverpool Citizen, 1889.

Moss, W: *The Liverpool Guide including a Sketch of the Environs, with a Map of the Town and Directions for Sea Bathing.* 3rd edition. J. McCreery, 1799.

Newsweek. Vol. 64, No 24, page 33, 14 December 1964.

Orchard, B. Guiness: *Liverpool's Legion of Honour.* Published by the Author, 1893.

The Parliamentary Sequestrators report of 1650 is in J. A. Picton, *Notes on the Origin and History of the Congregational Churches in Liverpool.* Benson & Holme, 1877.

Picton J. A: *Memorials of Liverpool* (2nd edition). Longmans, Green & Co., 1875 . Gilbert W. Walmsley, 1903.

The Porcupine. March 15 1862.

Priestley, J. B: *English Journey.* First published 1934. Heinemann, 1968.

Reilly, C. H: *Some Liverpool Streets and Buildings in 1921.* Liverpool Daily Post and Mercury, 1921.

Robinson, Ellen: *A Poem on seeing the Equestrian Statue of the late Majesty King George the Third to which is added a New Edition of Poems on seeing the Monument erected at Liverpool to the Honour and Memory of Lord Nelson, with Reflections on the Principal figures and also on the Burning of Moscow in 1812.* Printed for the author by A. Fleetwood, 1823.

Saxton, Eveline: 'School Lane' is in *Rhymes of Old Liverpool.* Liverpool Daily Post Printers, 1948.

Scott, Dixon: *Liverpool.* Painted by J. Hamilton Hay, described by Dixon Scott. Adam and Charles Black, 1907.

'A Sentimental Journey by a Lady' is in *The Lady's Magazine,* April 1775.

Shaw, Frank: *My Liverpool.* Wolfe Publishing Ltd, 1971.

Smith, Henry: *Liverpool.* Typescript in Liverpool Topographical Newspaper Cutting, page 139, Liverpool Local Studies Library [nd].

The Story of Lancashire. Edward Arnold, 1896.

The Story of Liverpool: The Second City of the Empire. The Albion Publishing Company, 1925.

The Stranger in Liverpool or an Historical and Descriptive View of the Town of Liverpool and its Environs. 7th Edition, T Kaye, 1823.

Taylor, Henry: *Old Halls in Lancashire and Cheshire including notes on the Ancient Domestic Architecture of the Counties Palatine.* J. E. Cornish, 1884.

Two Foreign Ladies give their Opinion of Liverpool is in *The Liverpool Review of Politics, Society, Literature, and Art.* 15 February 1890.

Vaughan, J. E: *A Brief View of Liverpool.* Typescript. Library Association Conference, Liverpool, 1966.

Wesley, John: *Journal,* 1775, quoted in *Liverpool, Evening Express,* February 8 1933.

Where to Go, What to See and Where to Stay in Liverpool. Official Handbook of the Holidays on Merseyside Association, 1934.

Whitty's Guide to Liverpool. Daily Post Steam Printing Works, 1871.

Whishaw, Francis: *The Railways of Great Britain and Ireland, Practically Described and Illustrated.* John Weale, 1842.

Williams, Peter Howell: *Liverpolitana: a Miscellany of People and Places.* Merseyside Civic Society, 1971.

Port Sunlight

Index

GROUNDCOVER
SERIES